SQUADRONS!

No. 40

THE NORTH AMERICAN
MUSTANG MK. III
OVER ITALY AND THE BALKANS (PT-1)

PHIL H. LISTEMANN

ISBN: 9791096490-64-6

Copyright

© 2020 Philedition - Phil Listemann

revised May 2024

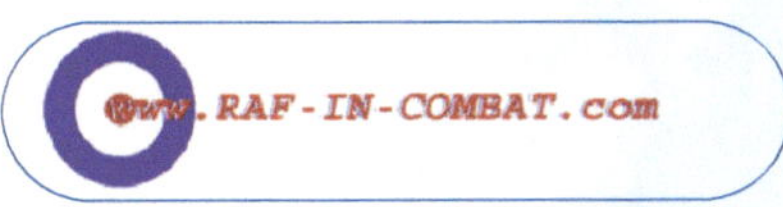

Colour profiles: Gaetan Marie/Bravo Bravo Aviation

PERSONEL :
(AUS)/RAF: Australian serving in the RAF
(BEL)/RAF: Belgian serving in the RAF
(CAN)/RAF: Canadian serving in the RAF
(CZ)/RAF: Czechoslovak serving in the RAF
(NFL)/RAF: Newfoundlander serving in the RAF
(NL)/RAF: Dutch serving in the RAF
(NZ)/RAF: New Zealander serving in the RAF
(POL)/RAF: Pole serving in the RAF
(RHO)/RAF: Rhodesian serving in the RAF
(SA)/RAF: South African serving in the RAF
(US)/RAF - RCAF : American serving in the RAF or RCAF

RANKS
G/C : Group Captain
W/C : Wing Commander
S/L : Squadron Leader
F/L : Flight Lieutenant
F/O : Flying Officer
P/O : Pilot Officer
W/O : Warrant Officer
F/Sgt : Flight Sergeant
Sgt : Sergeant
Cpl : Corporal
LAC : Leading Aircraftman

OTHER
ATA: Air Transport Auxiliary
CO : Commander
DFC : Distinguished Flying Cross
DFM : Distinguished Flying Medal
DSO : Distinguished Service Order
Eva. : Evaded
ORB : Operational Record Book
OTU : Operational Training Unit
PoW : Prisoner of War
PAF: Polish Air Force
RAF : Royal Air Force
RAAF : Royal Australian Air Force
RCAF : Royal Canadian Air Force
RNZAF : Royal New Zealand Air Force
SAAF : South African Air Force
s/d: Shot down
Sqn : Squadron
† : Killed

CODENAMES - OFFENSIVE OPERATIONS - FIGHTER COMMAND

CIRCUS:
Bombers heavily escorted by figthers, the purpose being to bring enemy figthers into combat.

RAMROD:
Bombers escorted by fighters, the primary aim being to destroy a target.

RANGER:
Large formation freelance intrusion over enemy territory with aim of wearing down enemy figthers.

RHUBARD:
Freelance fighter sortie against targets of opportunity.

RODEO:
A fighter sweep without bombers.

SWEEP:
An offensive flight by fighters designed to draw up and clear the enemy from the sky.

THE MUSTANG MK. III

The North American Mustang is certainly one of the legendary fighters of the Second World War. The aircraft can be split into two 'families', the Allison-powered and Merlin-powered. The RAF Marks I and II belong to the first category, while all subsequent marks belong to the second. The change of engine made the aircraft perform far better at higher altitudes. The Merlin 61 (with the two-stage supercharger) provided significantly improved results above 15,000 feet and was without compare above 20,000 feet. All this without sacrificing range. This was a key point as, in 1942, the RAF was looking for a long-range escort fighter, a role the Spitfire, whatever the mark, could not fulfill with complete satisfaction from the British Isles. The British conducted an experimental programme with the new engine on various test-beds (known within the RAF as the Mustang X) while the Americans were doing the same thing on their side. The Americans first discovered the best way to pair the Merlin and the airframe and, after the first flight of the XP-51B on 30 November 1942, the future of the P-51B was guaranteed. Many pre-orders were confirmed while the British soon requested an initial batch of 300 aircraft (**FB100-FB399**). The denomination allocated was 'Mustang III'. This would also apply to the P-51C the British later received. Indeed, the new model was in such high demand that a second production plant was opened at Dallas, Texas (P-51Bs built there were designated P-51Cs), while the P-51B was built at Inglewood, California. The first batch of Mustang IIIs was followed by a second of 250 airframes (**FX848-FZ197**), then a third for 141 airframes (**HB821-HB961**), while a last request for 450 was split between Mustang IIIs and Mustang IVs (See SQUADRONS! 10 & 11) with only the first 220 (**KH421 to KH640**) delivered as Mustang IIIs. Not all were delivered, however, as some crashed before delivery (FB205, FX992, HB920 and KH470). Deliveries were also dependent on US needs and, upon arriving on British soil, some Mustang IIIs were repossessed by the Americans to be later replaced by other P-51Bs and Cs from Eighth Air Force stocks, the replacement aircraft receiving serials **SR406 to SR440**.

From the start, deliveries did not entirely cover British needs and led to the order of some P-47 Thunderbolts (see SQUADRONS 2 & 23). Indeed, when the first Mustang IIIs were delivered at the end of 1943, the RAF was also looking to replace ageing and obsolescent Kittyhawks, serving in the Mediterranean theatre, and Hurricanes, in the Far East, and the Mustang was the first choice. The decision was made to give priority to western Europe and, consequently, the arrival of the first Mustang IIIs in the

A side view of Mustang III FX908. It belongs to a batch of P-51Bs intended to serve exclusively in the UK. Delivery started in November 1943. In 1945, with the high attrition of the type in the Middle East, the RAF had to send about a dozen UK-based Mustang IIIs to make up some of the shortfall. Only a few reached operational units before war's end. The ex-UK known to have arrived to Italy as reinforcement are FB128, FB145, FB149, FB170, FX862, FZ130 and FZ187 in March 1945, FB191, FB242, FX880, FX893, FX965 and FZ127 in April and FB124 in July.

While the Americans were working on their Merlin-powered version, the British did the same and called it the 'Mustang X'. It was the Americans who won the race with the P-51B having better performance than its counterpart across the Atlantic.

Mediterranean theatre took place in the middle of 1944, six months after the type had been introduced into service in the UK. For the Hurricane in the Far East, it was the Thunderbolt that was sent, pending the arrival of the next mark of Mustang. Of the 911 Mustang IIIs ordered, and 907 received, only 277, about a third, were sent directly to the Mediterranean, via Casablanca in French Morocco, to serve in the theatre. All were P-51Cs to ease maintenance and management of the spares stock:

P-51C-1-NT (from US batch 42-102979/103328)
FB244-FB343 (100)

P-51C-5-NT (from batch 42-103329/103778)
HB830, HB842, HB851, HB853, HB854, HB856, HB859, HB874, HB875, HB879-HB881, HB883, HB884, HB889 (15)

P-51C-10-NT (from batch 103779/103978 and 43-24902/25251, 44-10753/10782, 10818/10852, 44-10859/11036, 44-11123/11152)
HB892-HB917, HB919, HB921, HB922, HB924-HB929, HB931-HB933, HB935-HB941, HB943, HB945-HB948, HB950-HB953, HB955-HB958, HB960, HB961, KH427, KH428, KH437, KH456, KH459, KH461, KH463, KH465, KH467, KH468, KH472, KH475, KH476, KH486, KH487, KH496, KH501, KH512, KH513, KH520, KH522, KH530-KH534, KH538, KH543, KH544, KH549, KH553, KH560-KH562, KH568, KH571-KH573, KH575, KH576, KH579, KH583, KH586, KH587, KH589-KH598, KH600, KH601, KH603-KH640 (154).

The P-51C-5 and C-10 were equipped with the 1450hp V-1650-7 version of the Merlin, which was a bit more powerful than the V-1650-3 of the C-1 version (1400hp), but was also set to develop its power at medium altitudes instead of only high altitudes for the dash 3.

However, the Mustang III squadrons based in Italy operated over this country and the Balkans almost exclusively in the fighter-bomber role. After the liberation of Rome in June 1944, the presence of Axis (Luftwaffe and Italians still loyal to Mussolini) aircraft decreased considerably. The Mustang III, however, experienced high attrition and, by the spring of 1945, about 100 had been lost for one reason or another. Despite the introduction of the Mustang IV, the squadrons soon had to face a shortage in the supply of the type. Therefore, from February 1945, about a dozen ex-UK based Mustang IIIs were ferried to the region. The first began to reach operational units when the Germans and their allies in Italy surrendered. Up to May 1945, six squadrons were totally equipped with the type, No. 3 RAAF, No. 5 SAAF, and RAF 112, 213, and 249 Squadrons, while, just after the war, other units (RAF 250, 260, and the Australian 450) received a mix of Mustang IIIs and IVs. This first part will develop the operational usage of the dominion units (3 RAAF, 5 SAAF, 450) and the 'gift' units, 249 (Gold Coast) and 250 (Sudan) Squadrons. (Part 2 is developed in *SQUADRONS! 67*)

SUMMARY OF THE OPERATIONAL ACTIVITY OF THE MUSTANG III & IV IN ITALY 1944-45*

Squadron	Type	Sorties	Total per Sqn	Claims	Op. Losses	Acc. Losses	Losses
3 Sqn RAAF	Mk III	975		-	11	-	
	Mk IV	800	1,775	2.0	6	-	17
5 Sqn SAAF	Mk III	1,350		-	24	-	
	Mk IV	870	2,220	2.0	8	1	33
112 Sqn	Mk III	3,520		1.0	26	1	
	Mk IV	530	4,050	-	4	6	37
213 Sqn	Mk III	2,060		23.66	42	1	
	Mk IV	300	2,360	-	9	3	55
249 Sqn	Mk III	1,350		1.0	24	-	
	Mk IV	-	1,350	-	-	-	24
260 Sqn	Mk III	4,810		-	26	1	-
	Mk IV	-	4,810	-	-	-	27
Grand Total			16,565	31.66	180	13	193

** up to 30.09.45*

Below, Mustang FB260, inherited from Laurie Wilmot (see *SQUADRONS! 67*), with Eaton's personal insignia and his initials.

Brian Alexander EATON
AUS. 133

Brian Eaton was an Australian from Tasmania who enlisted in the RAAF in January 1936. By the outbreak of the war he was serving as a flying instructor. He remained in Australia until October 1942 when he sailed for North Africa and joined 3 Sqn, flying Kittyhawks, in January 1943 as a flight commander. Four months later he took over the unit and led it until March 1944 when he was rested, having been awarded a DFC in the meantime, and was made Companion of the DSO in April 1944 for his leadership. In August 1944, he returned to operational flying duty by taking command, as a group captain, of 239 Wing, replacing Lt-Col Wilmot. He led the wing until the end of the war and added a Bar to his DSO in June 1945. He remained in the RAAF, reaching the rank of Air-Vice Marshal, until retiring in December 1973.

North American Mustang Mk. III FB260
No. 239 Wing
Group Captain B.A. Eaton
Italy, autumn 1944

Victories - confirmed or probable claims: *nil*

First operational sortie:
29.11.44
Last operational sortie:
05.05.45

Number of sorties: *ca.* 975

Total aircraft written-off: 11

Aircraft lost on operations: 11
Aircraft lost in accidents: -

Squadron code letters:
CV

COMMANDING OFFICERS				
S/L Murray P. NASH	AUS. 400101	RAAF	...	08.03.45
F/L Kenneth A. RICHARDS (*Temp.*)	AUS. 400104	RAAF	08.03.45	03.05.45
S/L Murray P. NASH	AUS. 400101	RAAF	03.05.45	...

SQUADRON USAGE

Having served in the Mediterranean since the summer of 1940, this Australian unit had been almost constantly engaged on combat operations. By November of 1944, the squadron was based at Iesi in Italy and was commanded by S/L Murray P. Nash who had taken over the squadron the previous month. The squadron was, as were many fighter-bomber squadrons in the zone, equipped with the Curtiss Kittyhawk Mk.IV, which was at the end of its service life.

The winds of change came in the middle of November when the squadron was stood down to undertake conversion to the Mustang. While the first new aircraft had been taken on charge, they were all flown to Fano on the 18th where training continued. It is apparent the conversion was quick as the first operations were flown on the 22nd when the CO led a special op over the north of Italy, even though the Australians were not yet completely operational on the type. Practice flights continued over the next few days and the unit returned to operations on the 25th with a weather recce by two aircraft carrying 62-gallon long-range tanks under each wing. This kind of sortie was repeated the next day by the CO and W/O E.C. Jennings who completed the flight after remaining airborne

Two long-serving members of 3 Sqn and both DFC and Bar recipients. Left, Murray Nash, who arrived in January 1943 and commanded the squadron twice (until April 1944 and from October 1944 for his second tour). Ken Richards, right, completed two tours with the squadron - the first between August 1943 and October 1944 and the second from February 1945. He was awarded the DFC in March 1944, as was Nash, followed by a Bar in June 1945 while Nash received his Bar in July 1944. Nash was also awarded the DSO in August 1945.

A line-up of Mustangs of 3 Sqn at Fano in December 1944. Winter in northern Italy and the Balkans is very humid, rainy and foggy, and was a major issue for operations in the final stages of the war. Of the five Mustangs visible here, and identified, only KH593/CV-A would see 1945. The other four were lost: KH626/CV-Z and KH616/KH-diamond on 26.12.44, KH630/CV-C on 06.12.44, and KH623/CV-X on 15.12.44.

for five hours and ten minutes over Yugoslavia. The real first operation was eventually flown on the 29th when twelve aircraft attacked a railway line between Padua and Portogruaro. All twelve 500-lb bombs were dropped. While no direct hit was recorded, there were two near misses on the line with one more on the bridge. At the end of the month, the squadron was operating Mustangs FB262/T, FB283/W, KH522/K, KH593/A, KH615/B, KH616/diamond, KH617/L, KH618/J, KH624/Y, KH626/Z, KH630/C, KH631/V, KH632/G, and a sole Mk.IV (see *SQUADRONS! 11*).

December began with an armed recce of railways between Ferrara and Verona. Led by F/L I.H. Roediger, the six Mustangs were each carrying two 500-lb bombs. They found a stationary convoy on which they all dropped their bombs, but little damage was noticed. Free of bombs, the Mustangs continued on and a loco was heavily strafed and claimed as damaged. A truck and a trailer were attacked later and also claimed as damaged. A car was attacked and destroyed soon after. Over the next few days, 3 Squadron continued to carry out armed recces over Yugoslavia, performing one op a day when weather permitted (sometimes preceded by a weather recce). Numerous ground targets were found and many claims filed on return, the ideal targets being German vehicles. On the 6th, on return from an armed recce in the Brod-Sarajevo area, the formation of twelve Mustangs was forced to make a detour to avoid heavy cloud. When over the Adriatic, flying at 16,000 feet and above 10/10 cloud, the formation dived through cloud after receiving a homing to base. When they broke off, about 50 miles from the Italian coast, and at about 5000 feet, W/O R.E.R. Fountain was missing. He became the first Australian casualty since the conversion to the Mustang. Over the next few days, the weather did not improve and, while one successful armed recce was flown on the 11th, operational flying was limited to weather recces (when take off was possible). Finally, on the 15th, the weather improved enough and three ops were flown. With take offs at 08.45 and 08.50, two formations of six Mustangs reconnoitered different areas. The last op, flown in the afternoon (15.10), attacked and destroyed a road-river bridge at San Potito. On return, W/O Jennings ran off the runway and hit a bomb crater. His Mustang broke its back, but Jennings escaped injury. Over the next fortnight the weather was erratic and prevented flying most days. On the

The last-minute checks on the engine and the bugs fixed, Mustang KH624/CV-Y is taxiing for the runway guided with the help of a mechanic seated on the left wing. *(AHM of WA)*

The engine of Mustang III KH624/CV-Y receiving some attention, from mechanics at Fano, just before an operation. *(AHM of WA)*

25th, the Australians found trucks in the marshalling yards west of Celje. These were duly bombed from 1500 feet along the rails, but the Mustangs did not stay to see the results. Soon after, a fair amount of rail traffic was found moving in both directions, but no attacks were made as it was hoped to find the estimated 800 MTs reported in the area. The Mustangs found and strafed a loco and twenty vans instead. The loco was damaged and all the vans hit, as was a staff car found immediately after. Another train, using an engine at each end to push and pull, was hit and both engines stopped. This success was followed by another attack on yet another train, which was damaged, but all aircraft had to halt their attack after they ran out of ammunition. The next day, two ops were flown. While trying to take off, W/O R.G. Pedler was unable to lift off and crashed in the dispersal area. Fortunately, the bombs did not explode and he was only slightly injured. The aircraft was only good for scrap. The op was marred by bad luck as W/O B.J. Fay crashed on landing. Worse was yet to come, however. In the afternoon, while heading for the target, W/O J.F. Quinn, who was lagging behind the formation, was attacked by a single Bf109. Badly hit, the Mustang was seen spiraling down with white smoke coming from the engine. Quinn was seen to bale out. His Mustang, with bombs still attached, exploded in the fields nearby. Jack Quinn survived his parachute descent and friendly Italians hid him in vineyard farms for three weeks. However, an 'unfriendly' tipped off the Germans in early February 1945. He was captured and finished the war as a PoW, firstly in Italy and then in four camps in Germany. He was released on VE-Day. Quinn had been shot down by an ANR Bf109 2° *Gruppo Caccia* (*Capitano* Ugo Drago). Meanwhile, a second Bf109 came out of the sun to attack P/O Ken Caldecott, Quinn's attacker having pulled up hard and disappeared into the sun. This attack failed, however. Having dropped their bombs, the Australians could face this Bf109 and they began to patrol in the hope of catching him about to land. They were rewarded when the enemy aircraft was reported to be 4000 feet above at 9 o'clock. The Mustangs immediately turned and climbed. Flying Officer V.M. Thomas was the first to open fire, but made no claim. The Bf109 dived and the CO (in a Mustang IV) and his No.2, F/O W.A. Andrews, chased it at deck level across the southern boundary of Aviano aerodrome. They were able to overtake the Bf109 easily, but, owing to being so close to the ground, S/L Nash had difficulties in keeping a bead. He closed to 100 yards and fired three long bursts. The aircraft began to stream glycol. Andrews joined in the shooting, as he closed to 150 yards, until forced to pull away at 20 yards. He saw strikes on the left wing and cockpit and the Bf109's wheels were seen to come down. Thomas then came in and fired three bursts, but finally lost sight of the Bf109, which was not seen to crash. Therefore, it was claimed as damaged by the three pilots (records show the Bf109 did crash and was destroyed). More sorties were flown until the end of the month, with more ground claims forthcoming, and, despite severe losses, the tally for December stood at seven MTs, five rail trucks, two bridges, and a barge destroyed with many more probably destroyed and damaged. In January 1945, the Australians continued their destructive work. The Mustang IIIs were progressively succeeded by Mk.IVs as replacement aircraft (after a loss or when an aircraft had reached its airframe limit and was sent away for overhaul). Only one loss was recorded in January. On the 9th a formation of ten Mustangs (of which two were IVs), led by F/L J.A.T. Hodgkinson, took off to attack a road bridge over a river at Alfonsine (near Mestre). They arrived over the target at 8000 feet and bombed along the line of the bridge in a south-east direction from 1500 feet. The bridge received two direct hits, which demolished all of the southern span and most of the central span. Flying Officer Vincent M. Thomas, flying a Mk.III, went into a spin at 1500 feet after releasing his bombs. The aircraft crashed into a minefield and burst into flames. He may have been hit by flak. By the end of the month, the Mk.IIIs on charge were FB262/T, FB283/W, FB290/J, KH522/K, KH573/X, KH593/A, KH617/L, KH624/B (recently recoded), KH631/V, KH632/C (also recoded) and KH638/Z. The rest of the aircraft on strength were Mk.IVs. One Mustang III was lost during February. On the 21st, at 09.20, F/L Barney Davies led seven Mustangs to escort 450 Squadron

The pilot of Mustang KH618/CV-J ready to start the engine and taxi out for another op over the Balkans. Note the two 500-lb bombs hanging under the wings.
(AHM of WA)

Bombed up, Mustang III KH522/CV-K taxies out with the obligatory mechanic on the left wing. *(AHM of WA)*

Kittyhawks to bomb the Casarsa rail diversion. After 450 Squadron had bombed, the Mustangs bombed from east to west, diving to 1500 feet. Bombing was good, but no results were observed because of dusk and smoke. Warrant Officer Ian Rennison was seen to pull out slightly, when well in to his dive, and then go straight into the ground where the aircraft exploded. He had been posted in the month before after a few years of service with second line units. Padre Fred McKay searched for Rennison after the German surrender in May 1945 and conducted a proper burial service. Only a few February days were flyable for operations, just three days in the first fortnight, the second fortnight being much better. The squadron also made a move, heading to Cervia from the 26th.

In March the rhythm of operations accelerated and 3 Squadron carried out close to 450 sorties. It was also the first time the Mustang IV was used more than the Mk.III. The turnover of aircraft continued. While the Mk.IV was now the preferred choice, some older Mk.IIIs were also received. On 3 March, in the afternoon, the unit was briefed for flak suppression while 112 Squadron bombed the same morning's target at Casarsa. One 3 Squadron aircraft, flown by F/L J.A.T. Hodgkinson, had been holed during the morning sortie, but had been able to return to base. Flak was once more accurate and F/O D.D. Tennent was hit and reported he was in trouble. Hodginkson told him to climb and make for the coast. When Tennent was at about 2-3000 feet, thick white smoke and flames streamed back from his aircraft. He rolled his Mustang and baled out safely. The nature of the operations changed later in the month when the squadron was tasked with escorting Balkan Air Force medium bombers, usually Marauders, targeting Austria. The Luftwaffe was totally absent from these skies at that period of the war. At the end of March, Mustang IIIs FB252/X, FB290/J, KH593/A, KH624/E, KH631/V, KH632/C and KH638/Z were still flying with 3 Squadron. More than 630 sorties were flown in April, forty per cent of them flown by Mk.IIIs. Some old Mk.IIIs (FB244/V, FB299/Y, FB341/L and HB955/? - Question mark) were taken on charge that month instead of new Mk.IVs. FB299 had a very short career with the unit. On 14 April, G/C Eaton (Wing Leader 239 Wing) was leading a formation of six Mustangs to attack an enemy HQ position. Warrant Officer I.M. Redenbach was last seen going down in his bomb dive. He was initially posted missing, but soon after was reported to be held by

Mustang III KH624 was later recoded CV-B after KH615 was lost in January 1945. It is here seen bombed up. It retained the sky fuselage band and the rudder has been painted with the Southern Cross (in white on a blue rudder) as per the squadron's standard at the time. *(AHM of WA)*

the Germans as a PoW. He had been shot down by flak and was happy to have survived. During the same op, the squadron came close to losing a second Mustang as P/O K.R. Caldecott experienced trouble releasing one of his bombs. Even though he was told by Eaton to bale out over the sea, he decided to risk a landing, which he succeeded in doing. Actually, FB299 was the fourth Mustang III lost since the beginning of April. The previous day, W/O Ken Higgins had been posted missing after attacking a tank during a cab-rank sortie (these were called Ramrods in Fighter Command). After bombing, Higgins didn't rejoin the formation. He had been seen entering his bomb dive. Flying Officer A.F. Lane, the leader, went back below the clouds, to look for the telltale black smoke of a crashed aircraft, but found nothing. No distress call had been made by Higgins. He had actually crash landed five kilometres from the target, near the church at Sellustra. After the dive, he headed south, flying very low over the area of Casola Canina. Several people who saw him feared he would land right on their heads. Higgins crashed in a small field and uprooted some fruit trees. He got out of the Mustang with the help of local villagers and was observed to have broken some of his teeth in the forced landing. The local villagers still remember the event in great detail, such as the 'Australia' patches on the shoulders of his uniform, and that he was immediately taken prisoner by German airborne troops who were then withdrawing from the area. In fact, his captivity lasted only a few hours. During their retreat, the Germans left Higgins in an Italian medical centre where he was found by Allied personnel after liberation. His Mustang was treated quite differently; it was blown up by the German paratroopers after they had salvaged all of the available gasoline. Higgins was reported safe on 8 May 1945, but was then placed on the seriously ill list. Earlier in the month, on the 3rd, two Mustangs were shot down by flak on the second operation of the day, an armed recce over Yugoslavia with eight Mustangs led by F/L A.F. Shannon. The first to be shot down was W/O A. Clark. The leader had encountered a Fi156 and shot it down in flames (see *SQUADRONS! 11*), but Clark, acting as his number 2, was caught by flak and hit at 300 feet by 20mm cannon fire. He climbed to 5000 feet and baled out safely. The op continued and, soon after, a convoy of goods trucks was attacked. While strafing them W/O W.J. McInerheney was hit in the coolant tank. He climbed to 3000 feet and also baled out safely. Both pilots were saved by partisans. The end of war was approaching, however, and targets were few. Operations continued and the last ones were carried out on 1 and 2 May, both being shipping patrols, while all organised German resistance in Austria and Italy ceased at 12.00 on 2 May. However, some more shipping patrols were carried out the next day and the very last op, a recce of the Fiume, Trieste and Udine sector, was flown on the 5th. The same day, McInerheney rejoined the squadron, while Clark rejoined on 13 June. The squadron moved to Lavariano on the 18th, but not much happened during the following week as the squadron, after five years of service abroad, was not to stay in Europe. Personnel left for Naples, to embark for Australia, in August, leaving the Mustangs behind.

Date	Pilot	S/N	Origin	Serial	Code	Fate
06.12.44	W/O Ronald E.R. **Fountain**	Aus. 421195	RAAF	**KH630**	CV-C	†
15.12.44	W/O Edward C. **Jennings**	Aus. 412539	RAAF	**KH623**	CV-X	-
26.12.44	W/O Roy G. **Pedler**	Aus. 415951	RAAF	**KH634**	CV-E	-
	W/O Jack F. **Quinn**	Aus. 410420	RAAF	**KH616**	CV-J	PoW
09.01.45	F/O Vincent M. **Thomas**	Aus. 400944	RAAF	**KH615**	CV-B	†
21.02.45	W/O Ian **Rennison**	Aus. 419704	RAAF	**KH617**	CV-L	†
03.03.45	F/O David D. **Tennent**	Aus.429420	RAAF	**FB262**	CV-T	-
03.04.45	W/O Alan **Clark**	Aus. 432122	RAAF	**KH631**	CV-V	-
	W/O William J.F. **McInerheney**	Aus. 427718	RAAF	**FB290**	CV-J	-
13.04.45	W/O Tasman K. **Higgins**	Aus. 422522	RAAF	**KH638**	CV-Z	PoW
14.04.45	W/O Ian M. **Redenbach**	Aus. 419216	RAAF	**FB299**	CV-Y	PoW

Total: 11

Warrant Officer T.K. Higgins seen shortly before he was shot down and made a PoW on 13 April 1945. An Australian from New South Wales, he enlisted in the RAAF in May 1942. After completing his training, he served in second line units mostly, as a flying instructor, before being posted to 3 Sqn as his first operational assignment in September 1944. His captivity was short-lived however.

Below, Mustang KH631/CV-V in which W/O Clark was shot down. Note the Sky fuselage band has been overpainted. This recognition mark was progressively painted over, but the process was not complete when the war ended in Europe in May 1945.

Victories - confirmed or probable claims: 2.00

First operational sortie:
03.10.44

Last operational sortie:
02.05.45

Number of sorties: *ca.* 1350

Total aircraft written-off: 24

Aircraft lost on operations: 24
Aircraft lost in accidents: -

Squadron code letters:
GL

COMMANDING OFFICERS

Maj Thomas C. MacMurray *(PoW)*	SAAF No. 205667	SAAF	...	12.11.44
Maj David W. Murdoch	SAAF No. 205706	SAAF	14.11.44	20.03.45
Maj Hendrick O.M. Odendaal *(Eva.)*	SAAF No. 103164	SAAF	20.03.45	03.04.45
Maj Hillary J.E. Clarke *(†)*	SAAF No. 21685	SAAF	03.04.45	01.05.45
Capt Alan Q. de Wett *(Temp.)*	SAAF No. 48142	SAAF	01.05.45	20.05.45
Maj Hendrick O.M. Odendaal *(Eva.)*	SAAF No. 103164	SAAF	20.05.45	15.10.45

SQUADRON USAGE

Under RAF authority since February 1942, 5 Squadron SAAF had participated in the advance across the Western Desert to Italy. Equipped with the Kittyhawk Mk.IV, the unit was based at Iesi in Italy when the first Mustang IIIs were allocated at the end of September 1944. The officer commanding at the time was Maj T.C. MacMurray who had just assumed the role. The last Kittyhawk IV sortie was carried out on the 25th and then the pilots started the conversion to the Mustang. Aircraft FB251, FB256, FB275, FB289, HB839, HB909, HB914/D, HB921/B, HB931/X, HB939, HB947/A, KH456, KH486, KH487 and KH533 were added to the inventory within a couple of days. More than 100 hours were flown during the conversion process, which only lasted a couple of days. The first ops were carried on 3 October, the CO being the first to use the Mustang III during a morning ASR mission (with Lt K.C. Kemsley as wingman). Two armed recces followed in the afternoon. The next day of operations came on the 9th, following a short period of bad weather, with armed recces performed. The first cab-rank patrols, led by MacMurray, were flown late in the afternoon. The next day, Captains J.M. Pienaar and B.G.S. Enslin were dispatched for an early afternoon weather recce. After they had passed the weather reports on, and having no further instructions, they had set course for base when they spotted MTs. They went down to strafe, but Enslin soon after lost track of Pienaar who was eventually posted missing. Hit by ground fire, he had to make a forced landing and was eventually taken prisoner. He was the first of 5 Squadron's operational losses on the Mustang. Sorties continued over the next few days (more cab-ranks) and included specifically assigned ground targets, like on the 12th when an ammunition dump was attacked and destroyed. The next day it was a bridge that was targeted, but flak damaged the Mustang flown by Lt A.W. Mitchell. On 15 October, the squadron was dispatched to try to locate guns north of Cesena. Lieutenant G. Murray, who had joined the month before, was last seen in his bombing dive. He was posted missing believed killed. In the second part of October the number of daily sorties increased significantly. The rest of the month was uneventful if we ignore that another Mustang (Lt E.R. Borland) was slightly damaged by flak on the 25th while attacking a railway line. More than 225 sorties were flown in October.

November was split in two halves. Initially, the South Africans operated from Iesi, while, from the 19th, the squadron flew from Fano. Weather over the region was wet and humid, but permitted the squadron to conduct many sorties – 300. November, however, was a very costly month. It started badly on the first day when Capt K.C. Kemsley, flight commander and leading eleven Mustangs, was hit by ground fire while attacking a locomotive in the area of Venice and crashed. He was replaced by Lt W. Lombard two days later. In the afternoon, Lt R.W.P. Manning was lost in the same circumstances, but over Yugoslavia, and was seen to crash into a hill after his aircraft was hit. He was thought to have been killed, but he survived. Indeed, as Manning was about to jump, the Mustang went into a

Thomas Cargill MacMurray

SAAF No. 205667

From Durban, South Africa, Tom MacMurray enlisted in the SAAF in December 1940. He completed his training in South Africa, at the end of which, in January 1942, he was posted to No. 10 Squadron SAAF based in the Union flying Mohawks. In September, he headed north to join the Desert Air Force and was posted to No. 5 Squadron SAAF equipped with Tomahawks, then Kittyhawks, from January 1943, becoming a flight commander in December. Tour-expired in March 1944, he returned to operations in June, performing the same role with the same squadron, before assuming command in September, overseeing the conversion to the Mustang III. On 12 November, operating over the Balkans, he was shot down while attacking a train and crashed. Captured, but severely wounded, his left leg was eventually amputated. Liberated at the end of the war, MacMurray was finally released from service in May 1946.

North American Mustang Mk. III KH622
No. 5 Squadron, SAAF
Cervia (Italy), spring 1945

spin, throwing him back into the cockpit. Having lost height, it was too late to bale out so the only thing left to do was a forced landing. No longer strapped in, bringing the aircraft down to earth was certainly hazardous. He survived and was saved almost immediately by partisans. Manning was eventually evacuated to a hospital in Italy with a broken leg. The next day, no operations were carried out and, on the 3rd, two armed recces, by six aircraft each, were flown in the morning on two axes: the railways between Brod and Sarajevo and those between Zagreb and Maribor. While some locos were found and strafed, the peak came when the second formation strafed an aerodrome near Zagreb. No less than three Ju52s were claimed as destroyed on the ground with three more and a Ju87 damaged. The aerodrome was well defended, however, and flak hit Lt Borland's Mustang which crashed and exploded on the field. The next day, Lt C.C. Begg sighted a Ju52 near Sarajevo during an armed reconnaissance and he shot it down on flames with a long burst from 150 yards closing in to 50 yards. Two days later on the 6th, it was the turn of Lt R.R. Linsley to be shot down while attacking an armoured train in a marshalling yard at Sarajevo. He was seen to crash his Mustang nearby. On 9 November, Lieutenants C.G. Begg and R.G.P. Osler set course for the Balkans for a weather recce over Yugoslavia. The weather did not behave so they turned for home, encountering a Ju52 soon after. Conrad Begg closed in, to make sure the tri-motor was in enemy use, while the crew was already firing at him and hitting the Mustang's wing and tail. Breaking away, Begg jettisoned his long-range tanks and attacked from about 15° from astern as the Junkers was dived for the cover of a rainstorm. Opening fire at 400 yards, Begg closed to 200 yards, setting the fuselage and right engine on fire. The Ju52 broke up and crashed on the side of a mountain. This victory and the claim made on the 4th was met with great enthusiasm, as the squadron hadn't scored for a long time, but was short-lived as, on the 12th, two pilots were posted missing. Both were shot down during the same op, an early armed recce during which locos were attacked. Both pilots were seen to bale out. Lieutenant D.H.R. MacLeod, the second pilot to be shot down, was rescued by partisans and was back with the squadron the following month. Major Tom MacMurray, the CO, was captured, severely wounded, and had to have a leg amputated. His position was taken over by Capt D.W. Murdoch, a flight commander, whose old position was in turn assumed by Lt H.J.E. Clarke two days later. The last loss of the month occurred on the 21st when Lt B.J. Eaton was last seen in a dive to bomb a bridge and houses at Faenza. It was his first operational flight. November was a very deadly month for the South Africans. Lieutenant P.M.C. Israel also died in hospital from injuries sustained in not relative flying accident.

With all these losses, it was logical to see a great influx of pilots to not only replace the ones lost, but also the ones who were tour-expired and sent back to the Union. It was the same for the aircraft and the first Mustang IVs were taken on charge. While November had been tough, December was worse! On 1 December, Capt W.J. Lombard led a 5 Squadron formation of twelve Mustangs across the Po Valley on an armed recce to interdict ground traffic. A bridge was eventually bombed followed by a strafing of MTs at low level, too low maybe as Lt C. Coetzer's left wing struck a tree and he crashed in flames. The squadron continued its destructive sorties over Yugoslavia, claiming various targets as destroyed or damaged, while, on the 4th, the Mustang IV was sent on operations for the first time (see *SQUA-*

An unidentified Mustang III, coded GL-N, of 5 Sqn seen at a RSU after it had been damaged in a belly landing (as seen by the bent propeller). The Sky fuselage band has been painted out. *(S. Bouwer)*

If USAAF standards of the time were followed, this very much weathered and patched Mustang III, KH622/GL-I, would have been classed as 'war-weary' and long withdrawn from use, but Lt T. Jones chose to retain the unit's last Mustang III until it ran out of airframe hours. Being faster at sea level than the Mk.IV, the Mk.III was preferred by some South African pilots. Note the Zulu Impi shield painted under the cockpit. Terry Jones continued to serve in the SAAF until his retirement in 1984.
(S. Bouwer)

DRONS! 11). During this same op, Lt F. Lock, a new replacement, was shot down by ground fire while attacking MTs near Brod. Lock managed to bale out and survived as a PoW. Two days later, ten Mustangs took off led by Lombard. The two other squadrons of 239 Wing were also part of the show and the target was a heavy concentration of rail and road traffic near Brod. The weather was very poor to the point that one squadron turned back, but the South Africans and the Australians of 3 Squadron persisted. In the end, a U-turn order was given and the South Africans set course for base after two hours. However, it soon became impossible for the formation to stay together. Bombs and long-range tanks were jettisoned over the sea. At that moment, Capt Lombard called up and told the other pilots to rendezvous under the cloud, as did Lt P.G. MacGuire and Captain A. de Wet, but the other pilots returned to base independently section by section. Then disaster came. Caught by very poor weather, many pilots became lost or disorientated in cloud. Lieutenant G.D. Kilpin was nearly into Switzerland when he ran out of fuel and baled out. He spent the rest of the war as a PoW. Lieutenant A.E. Burnett did the same near Lovinac, but got lucky as he was saved by partisans and brought to Udbina LG where he was surprised to find a SAAF Beaufighter of 16 Squadron on a special mission. He was flown back to Italy the following day. Four pilots, however, were killed: Capt Lombard (in the Mk IV), and Lieutenants T.F. Hart, C.G. Begg and E.W. Hall, the latter having managed to bale out. Another Mustang was damaged by Lt R.G.P. Osler when he stressed its wings leveling out from a spiral dive as he emerged from cloud. A logical court of inquiry was set up to learn what exactly had happened that day. Over the next few days, following such losses, the squadron maintained a reduced operational activity, but that did not prevent further loss. On the 11th, Lt W.N. Spence was shot down and killed by ground fire while attacking a train north of Sarajevo. Fortunately for the South Africans, they were mostly inactive for the next few days because of bad weather. The time was used to recover. The Mustang III remained the main type in use as the introduction of the Mk.IV was slow despite the heavy losses. The unit's contribution was far from negligible, however, with 267 500-lb bombs, 24 1000-lb and 9 napalm bombs dropped (from both Mk.IIIs and Mk.IVs) and numerous targets claimed as either destroyed or damaged.

After two rough months, January proved to be quiet, at least until the last few days. Operations were hampered by bad weather and no losses were recorded until the 23rd. That day, Capt 'Nobby' Clarke took off with ten Mustangs (seven being Mk.IIIs) to bomb a bridge at Zagreb. At the target, one Mustang, probably the one flown by Capt Enslin (a Mk.IV), was seen to go down in flames, while Lt J. van Rensburg, one of the newcomers, was last seen in his bombing dive. Three other Mustangs were damaged by flak. To hardly balance those losses, one direct hit was obtained at the northern end, buckling the lattice girder type bridge, two direct hits were scored on the track northwards, destroying 45 metres of it, and one hit destroyed track at the southern end. The remaining fighters strafed many railway trucks and locos and left two armoured cars smoking. The squadron then flew a successful op on the 25th before a halt due to poor weather, returning to operations on the 30th with an armed recce in the Gemona-Udine-Gorizia-Trieste area. Targets of opportunity were found and bombed with a railway line cut before its locos were taken care of and a barge strafed. Lieutenant G. Redman was hit

The last two OCs of 5 Sqn were Maj H.O.M. Odendaal, left, and Maj H.J.E. Clarke. Clarke took over from Odendaal when the latter was shot down in a Mustang IV on 3 April 1945, two days after he took command. He managed to evade capture and resumed his position in May. His successor had less luck as he was shot down on 1 May, in a Mustang IV, to become the last SAAF operational loss of the war. 'Oddie' Odendaal, a regular SAAF officer, continued his career and participated in the Korean conflict with 2 Squadron SAAF before retiring as a brigadier. *(Odendaal family left, M. Schoeman, right)*

by ground fire and managed to bale out north-west of Trieste. He was captured. During the month, the balance between the Mk.IIIs and Mk.IVs began to change and, by the end of the month, Mk.IIIs represented little more than half of the squadron's fleet. The Mk.III had been the workhorse for the South Africans that month.

Due to bad weather, February began with little operational activity. Almost all of the ops were flown with 1000-lb bombs. On the 21st, Capt H.O.M. Odendaal led an attack on the Dogna rail bridge. There was haze over the target, but the South Africans attempted to attack despite the reduced visibility as no alternative target had been provided. Odendaal accompanied the last Mustang to dive on it, seeing Lt J. Potgieter's Mustang catch fire and crash. The next day, the 22nd, Lt R. Condon experienced engine trouble on return to base from a bombing sortie. The engine eventually cut and he had to force land before he could reach base. He was saved, but the Mustang was a write-off. The next day, the squadron moved to Cervia. All ops until the end of the war in Europe were carried out from there. It

Mustang III KH620/GL-O parked with bombs under the wings. The serial has disappeared under the overpainted Sky fuselage band, but it is believed to be KH592, one of the last Mustang IIIs on charge at war's end. *(M. Schoeman)*

Mustang III KH610/GL-C seen before it was lost on 23 April 1945. It was last seen with its pilot, Lt 'Jock' Muir, pulling out of his bombing dive south of the Po River.
(M. Schoeman)

did not take time for another pilot to be posted missing. Lieutenant R. Flak, who had only joined a week before, did not return from an attack on a stores dump north of Lake Cammachio on the 26th. It was presumed he had been shot down by flak. The number of Mk.IIIs on hand continued to fall and by the end of February only KH475/X, KH533, KH562/R, KH605/W, KH610/C, KH611, KH620/O and KH622/I continued to be used.

March was a very busy and successful month. There was also a change of command, when Capt Odendaal replaced the tour-expired Maj Murdoch on the 20th. An immediate DFC was also awarded to Lt R. Turner who, despite a very short time on ops, 14 hours, had already distinguished himself. While attacking a fuel dump on 10 March in Mustang III KH607, he was hit in the chest by small arms fire and severely wounded. Then, although his left collarbone and arm had been broken and he had lost a considerable amount of blood, he flew his machine back to base and carried out a successful landing. Even though more than half the procedures required for landing had to be performed with the left hand, he operated the flap mechanism by using his broken left arm as a lever, putting the weight of his body on the arm to depress the lever. No loss was sustained in March. This was a first since conversion to Mustangs. Also for the first time, the Mk.IV finally took most of the operational load. Weather was fairly good in April, making numerous sorties possible even though the whole front was collapsing. Despite this, the Germans and their allies were still offering determined resistance in some places. The squadron sustained some losses, including the CO (who was replaced by newly-promoted Maj D. Clarke), but these were initially limited to the Mk.IVs. The Mustang IIIs were preserved until the 19th. That day, 5 Squadron flew five cab-ranks, including two attacks on tanks. The first loss was the squadron's senior flight commander, Capt J.C. Coetzee, in a Mustang IV. It was not long until the next loss. Major Clarke and Lt D.R. Hattingh took off on a Rover and successfully bombed a strongpoint. Hattingh, who had been taking photographs for South African Public Relations, radioed that he had been hit. He was seen to bale out behind enemy lines and was eventually captured with a badly burnt leg and taken to a German field hospital. Some Italians helped him escape and reach partisans soon after. He managed to regain Allied lines and was taken to a New Zealand hospital within nine days. The last Mk.III loss a few days later was reported at the time the Allies had reached the Po River. Lieutenant P. Muir, who was almost at the end of his tour, was last seen pulling out of his bombing dive while attacking ferry terminals near Venice. At the end of April, the squadron was almost fully re-equipped with the Mk.IV, with the Mk.IIIs, clearly in a back-up role, flying a third of the ops for the month. The Mk.IIIs still on charge were FB242, FB325, FZ187 and KH592. In May the Mk.IIIs participated in ops on the 1st and 2nd (during which Maj Clarke was lost in a Mk.IV), but not on the unit's last operation of the war the following day. The squadron moved to Lavariano on 10 May where its personnel waited for repatriation to the Union by disbandment of the squadron in October.

5 Sqn flying in a large V formation. While the majority of the Mustangs are Mk.IVs, some Mk.IIIs were still on strength, as seen by KH620/GL-O and KH605/GL-W on the far right, and a third one to the far left (possibly GL-A). The aircraft leading is KH692/GL-D, the Mustang usually flown by Maj Clarke who was shot down and killed in this aircraft on 1 May 1945. *(S. Bouwer)*

Date	Pilot	SN	Origin	Type	Serial	Code	Nb	Cat.
06.11.44	Lt Conrad G. **Begg**	SAAF No. 103548	SAAF	Ju52	**KH456**	GL-M	1.0	C
09.11.44	Lt Conrad G. **Begg**	SAAF No. 103548	SAAF	Ju52	**KH603**	GL-A	1.0	C

Total: **2.00**

Date	Pilot	S/N	Origin	Serial	Code	Fate
10.10.44	Capt Jacobus M. **Pienaar**	SAAF No. 328996	SAAF	**KH486**		PoW
15.10.44	Lt Gavin C. **Murray**	SAAF No. 543040	SAAF	**FB251**		†
01.11.44	Capt Keith C. **Kemsley**	SAAF No. 103588	SAAF	**HB950**		†
	Lt Reginald W.P. **Manning**	SAAF No. 543280	SAAF	**HB935**		Eva.
03.11.44	Lt Ernest R. **Borland**	SAAF No. 542782	SAAF	**HB939**		†
06.11.44	Lt Reginald R. **Linsley**	SAAF No. 542450	SAAF	**KH487**		†
12.11.44	Maj Thomas C. **MacMurray**	SAAF No. 205667	SAAF	**KH456**	GL-M	PoW
	Lt Donald H.R. **McLeod**	SAAF No. 542299	SAAF	**FB289**		Eva.
21.11.44	Lt Brian J. **Eaton**	SAAF No. 205799	SAAF	**HB909**		†
01.12.44	Lt Cornelius J. **Coetzer**	SAAF No. 542665	SAAF	**FB275**		†
04.12.44	2/Lt Frank N. **Lock**	SAAF No. 104001	SAAF	**HB914**	GL-D	PoW
06.12.44	Lt Thomas F. **Hart**	SAAF No. 542470	SAAF	**HB931**	GL-X	†
	Lt Conrad G. **Begg**	SAAF No. 103548	SAAF	**KH576**		†
	Lt Ewart W. **Hall**	SAAF No. 543049	SAAF	**KH607**	GL-L	†
	Lt Geoffrey D. **Kilpin**	SAAF No. 206329	SAAF	**FB301**		PoW
	Lt Alan E. **Burnett**	SAAF No. 103833	SAAF	**FB256**		Eva.
11.12.44	Lt William N. **Spence**	SAAF No. 543137	SAAF	**FB247**		†
23.01.45	Lt Daniel J.J. van **Rensburg**	SAAF No. 542743	SAAF	**KH587**	GL-E	†
30.01.45	Lt George L. **Redman**	SAAF No. 542906	SAAF	**KH603**	GL-A	PoW
21.02.45	Lt John W. **Potgieter**	SAAF No. 98509	SAAF	**HB947**		†
22.02.45	Lt Roy L. **Condon**	SAAF No. 103725	SAAF	**KH562**		-
26.02.45	Lt Roydon H.R. **Flack**	SAAF No. 103661	SAAF	**KH533**		†
19.04.45	Lt Derrick R. **Hattingh**	SAAF No. 543233	SAAF	**FB264**		Eva.
23.04.45	Lt Percy **Muir**	SAAF No. 103295	SAAF	**KH610**	GL-C	†

Total: **24**

Victories - confirmed or probable claims: 1.00

First operational sortie:
13.09.44
Last operational sortie:
13.04.45

Number of sorties: *ca.* 1350

Total aircraft written-off: 24

Aircraft lost on operations: 24
Aircraft lost in accidents: -

Squadron code letters:

GN

COMMANDING OFFICERS

S/L Jack Te Kloot	Aus. 414276	RAAF	...	02.12.44
S/L Charles E. Edmondson	Aus. 402326	RAAF	02.12.44	02.06.45
F/L Thomas H.E.B. Ashworth *(Temp.)*	RAF No. 127886	RAF	02.06.45	16.08.45

SQUADRON USAGE

A fighter unit that distinguished itself during the siege of Malta, the squadron, by the end of the summer of 1944, was equipped with the venerable, but totally obsolete, Spitfire Mk.V. The squadron was based at Canne, Italy, and had an Australian CO, S/L Jack Te Kloot. It had joined the Balkan Air Force in July before embarking on a considerable number of fighter-bomber sorties over the Balkans. The Mustang, with its longer range, was more suited to this role. Thus conversion became a necessity.

The first Mustangs arrived at the end of August. About two weeks were allowed for the pilots to undertake conversion. Operations with the Spitfires were not hampered, just reduced, during this period. Training was carried out with HB924/D, HB928/A, HB933/X, HB937, HB941, HB944, HB946/E, HB952/F, HB976, KH422, KH425, KH428, KH437, KH465, KH468, and KH476, the Mustangs that had been taken on charge by September. The squadron's first operations with the Mustang took place from Brindisi, a regular advanced base, when, at first light on the 13th, Te Kloot and 2/Lt W. Shields were airborne for a sortie along the Vardar River Valley. They crossed the Albanian coast near Mifol and flew east towards the Salonika region, where they turned north, following the course of Vardar to Krilovak and Veles, strafing suitable targets. They eventually damaged four locomotives, an armoured car and a railway wagon. A second operation was flown in the middle of the afternoon by the same team. Once more they crossed the Albanian coast north of Sarandë, near the Greek border, bypassed Ioannina and Karditsa, Greece, covering the road towards Larissa. Close to Taousani, west of Larissa, they attacked a convoy of about twenty vehicles going north and left one M/T burning and another damaged. Then they turned south of Almiros and headed to Domokos. On the road from Domokos to Lamia they came across a convoy of several hundred M/T moving north. They made two attacks, but 2/Lt Shields' Mustang suffered damage to its glycol system. He climbed to 12,000 feet and flew southwest before baling out about 10 miles south-east of Agrinio. Fortunately, upon reaching the ground, he was helped by Greek partisans and was back at Taranto on 21 October, despite being ill, and returned to the squadron in January 1945. The introduction of the Mustang was tough with the loss of one aircraft, on its first day of operations with the type, and one pilot out of action for a while. Over the next few days, operations were flown at a low rate while training continued for the pilots not yet operational on the Mustangs. On 19 September, three Mustangs led by Capt R.T. Whittingham (SAAF) went on a Rhubarb during which they attacked trains and the airfield at Larissa. On return they claimed one Fw190 and Ju52 damaged on the ground, with four locomotives destroyed and two more damaged, plus 21 MTs damaged, and one barge-mounted crane severely damaged. Whittingham returned to Larissa the next day with F/L A.E. Dryden (RNZAF). They claimed two Ju52s destroyed, a Ju88 and Bf109 damaged, five locos destroyed and three more damaged. The next day, Sgt A.W. Manning, while attacking the same aerodrome, was hit by flak in several places, including the rudder, fuselage and radiator, and lost his hood after having destroyed a Ju52 on the ground (his leader, F/O T.H.E.B. Ashworth, made the same claim). Manning managed to move away from Larissa, but the aircraft was too damaged to continue flying safely so he was obliged to bale out. Here too, he was saved by Greek partisans, and was back in Allied hands a few days later, but did not return to the squadron. After a short stay at hospital, he was posted to the UK. The squadron was in a run of bad luck as the next day, the 22nd, F/L A.E. Dryden was killed in a crash after the train he attacked blew up. He was apparently hit by debris and must have lost control. Captain Whittingham, who was flying

Jack Te Kloot
Aus. 414276

Enlisting in the RAAF in August 1941, Te Kloot completed his training in Australia and sailed for overseas operations at the end of July 1942 with a commission. He arrived in the UK in October 1942 and initially served in second-line units until May 1943 when he was posted to Malta where he joined No 229 Squadron. In January 1944, he was posted to No 185 Squadron as a flight commander and, in May, moved to No 249 (Gold Coast) Squadron to command. He led 249 until the end of his tour in December. He was made a Companion of the DSO upon leaving. No further operational positions followed and he was repatriated to the UK in April 1945 for repatriation to Australia in July, leaving the service in December.

North American Mustang Mk. III HB946
No. 249 (Gold Coast) Squadron
Canne (Italy), autumn 1944

In autumn 1944, 249 Sqn operated behind German lines in northern Greece with a detachment based at a secret airfield at Deskori. Here, Mustang III HB946/GN-E is being camouflaged. This airfield was codenamed 'Piccadilly Peggy'. *(Andrew Thomas)*

with Dryden, circled the area searching for his missing wingman and, in doing so, took the opportunity to attack more trains. On his last strafing run, he was also damaged by debris, as he overflew his victim, and flew away losing coolant. The South African set course for base, climbing to 12,000 feet, but the engine soon seized so he baled out. Helped by Greek partisans, he was back with the squadron unscathed by that evening. So far, 249 had been engaged in strafing missions, but, on the 24th, the first bombing sortie was carried out with six aircraft. The target was a gun position, which was duly worked over. No loss was sustained for a change, probably due to the lack of flak. The squadron, however, suffered another loss on the 27th when F/Sgt Edgar Ray (RAAF) was shot down by flak while attacking MTs. He was seen baling out, but it seems his 'chute failed to open. September ended with a new kind of op, an escort for a single Lysander on a SOE mission (Townbucket mission) completed by Flying Officers G.C. Nichols and J.R. Muir. September had been a deadly month with five Mustangs lost on operations and two pilots killed in only 63 sorties. It was far from an auspicious beginning!

In October, the rhythm of operations increased slightly, with 117 sorties flown, but the loss ratio remained high. On 8 October two Mustangs, flown by 2/Lt H.K. Rachmann (SAAF) and F/O D.P.F. McCaig, were airborne from Brindisi for a strafing sweep along the railways from Edessa to Veria, then to Llanovergi and Eleotherokhorion on the west coast of the Thermaic Gulf. The op was quiet and had so far only encountered some light, inaccurate flak near a viaduct under repair. Then the pair attacked a motor vehicle, with no results, and continued on until both were caught by light flak near Gefyra, east of Pella. The Mustang flown by Dennis McCaig, a Fijian, was apparently hit, but not immediately noticed. It was a bit later that McCaig found he was losing glycol. He tried to climb, but the stream of white vapour, which had appeared previously, intensified and the engine stopped after it sputtered twice. McCaig decided to bale out. He was rescued by friendly people on the ground and later handed to British agents. On 16 October, Capt Whittingham appeared to have suffered a glycol leak just after attacking a locomotive pulling two wagons, although no flak was seen during the attack. The section set course for Biferno, but Whittingham had to bale out about five miles northeast of the Tremiti Isles. He saw his aircraft falling into the sea with its engine on fire. He managed to get into his dinghy and was later rescued by a Catalina. On the 19th W/O C.N.V. Davey was lost returning from a bombing sortie in northern Greece, He became lost with P/O R. Andrew due to bad weather. Andrew managed to bale out after running out of fuel, and was reported safe three days later, but Davey was posted missing. Sadly, five days later, 2/Lt H.K. Rachmann was seen to hit the ground while attacking a convoy. It was never determined if the light flak experienced was responsible for the crash or if it was a case of pilot error. On 30 October, 249, with three Mustangs, flew with four aircraft from 213 Squadron. Led by G/C MacDonald, and coming down through clouds, the formation became separated from the leader and did not join up with him again. Flying Officer Geddes, having lost the formation, heard MacDonald calling, but was unable to find him and decided to return to base. The other five Mustangs flew north to Skopje where a stationary convoy was attacked, during which a 213 Mustang was shot down. The remaining four aircraft returned too, but encountered a severe storm south of Vis. Sergeant H.G. Pallett was heard to say he would bale out and was last seen 10 miles south-east of Lagosta Island. Searches for him during the next two days proved fruitless. The next day, the last day of October, F/L P.F. Noble and F/O J. Dickerson set out at dawn on an armed reconnaissance. They crossed the coast near

Divjakë and then flew over the lakes to Floriana and swept along the Bitol-Prilep and Durazzo-Scutari roads. No MTs were sighted. North of Bitol, however, they encountered a low-flying Fi156. Noble was the first to open fire and Dickerson followed from a different angle, closing rapidly, and managed to get in a brief, optimistic burst of fire, at a narrow deflection angle, without obvious results before overshooting and pulling round sharply to avoid the side of the forested valley. As he came round, he looked back and saw the Storch had struck the hillside. There was no fire or explosion and the wings were folded back over a bent fuselage. The two pilots shared what would be the squadron's 328th, and last, aerial victory of the war.

Throughout November and December 1944, 249, as with the entire Balkan Air Force, concentrated on transport targets to prevent the Germans from escaping. Despite bad weather until the end of the year, the squadron was able to increase the number of sorties flown, with 137 in November and 274 in December. Good results against MTs were obtained and losses were thankfully light. On 12 November, four Mustangs were tasked for an amred rece over Knin area. While taking off, the left wheel of the Mustang flown by Sgt J.R. Davie went into a hole filled with water, mud and sand causing the Mustang to swing to the left and overshot the end of the runway; the Mustang was finally stopped by sand at edge of it. Lucky was Davie as the two 500-lb bombs under the wings did not explode. The three remaining Mustangs led by F/O T. Ashworth continued their mission without incident to report on return. On 24 November, Sgt P.W. Amis experienced an oil leak and engine failure on returning from a sortie. He decided to bale out in to the sea about 50 miles east by north of Biferno. His three colleagues saw him get into his dinghy and continued to circle until he was picked up by an ASR Catalina. A few days later, 2/Lt A.J. Malherbe (SAAF) and Sgt W.J. Monkman were briefed to fly an armed weather recce to the area of Podgorica. On return they were caught by bad weather and Malherbe lost sight of Monkman and landed at Vis alone. It was later discovered Monkman had baled out near Split and was safely on his way back to Italy. Less luckier was Sgt F.J. Weed who was posted missing after attacking a road bridge near Bioce. He was later reported a prisoner of war. On 27 December it was the turn of F/Sgt M. Smith to experience some misadventure when, while attacking a convoy with F/O J.R. Muir, he was hit in the glycol system by intense flak. Smith managed to evacuate his aircraft, after its engine cut out, and landed safely. He started walking down a mountain slope and eventually rejoined the unit, with the help of partisans, within a few days. Two days later, F/O J.W. Gardner swung on take-off for an armed weather recce. Hitting the sand bank alongside the strip, he was lucky to escape injury as there was no fire, or explosion from the two 500-lb bombs under the wings. The Mustang, however, was only good for scrap. December ended with a new CO as S/L Te Kloot was replaced by another Australian, S/L C.E. Edmonson, on 2 December. The first half of January proved unsuitable for anything but training flights. The second half saw the weather improve, but only 150 sorties had been performed by the end of the month. The only loss for January occurred on the 26th when, returning from a successful sortie (during which nine Mustangs, led by F/L J.R. Muir, claimed no less than eight locos destroyed or damaged, and 175 wagons destroyed or damaged), F/Sgt P.C. Jones crashed landed at Vis and overturned. The pilot escaped with minor injuries.

The improved weather in February made it possible for 249 to fly nearly double the number of sorties of the previous month. On 2 February, six Mustangs led by the CO flew an armed reconnaissance to the area of Dravograd, Celje, Maribor and Zagreb, thus

Squadron Leader Te Kloot, with bush hat, stands with some of his pilots at 'Piccadilly Peggy' in September 1944. *(Andrew Thomas)*

Charles Edward Edmondson
Aus. 402326

After training in Australia, Edmondson sailed for the Middle East in the middle of 1941 and, after attending No 71 Operational Training Unit in Egypt, was posted to No 451 (RAAF) Squadron, a tactical reconnaissance unit, in August. He ended his tour in September 1943 and was posted the following month to No 260 Squadron, then to No 225 Squadron in December where he stayed until February 1944. Edmondson returned to operations at the end of October as a flight commander with No 249 (Gold Coast) Squadron, the aim being to eventually assume command of the unit. He remained at its head until June 1945 and was repatriated soon after with a DSO awarded in December that year.

North American Mustang Mk. III KH427
No. 249 (Gold Coast) Squadron
Canne (Italy), autumn 1944

approaching the Austrian border with Yugoslavia. Their target was the railway bridge at Laško, south of Selje, on the line from Austria to northern Italy. After they made their attack, which included several near misses, they continued on trying to find targets of opportunity. Soon after, rolling stock was strafed along the railway system north-west of Zagreb to Celje and north to Maribor where considerable flak was experienced, hitting Sgt Monkman's Mustang in the fuselage. Lieutenant R.V. Jacobs was not so lucky as he was shot down and killed. The following days were free of events of note until the 26th. In the morning, two Mustangs, led by F/O D.P.F. McCaig, took off for a weather recce along the Dalmatian coast. They were also tasked to check if a vessel, recently claimed as destroyed by SAAF Beaufighters in Fiume harbour, had been really sunk. McCaig flew below a thin layer of stratus cloud with a base at 5000 feet. Visibility did not exceed 10 miles. He then flew low over the harbour looking for signs of the vessel, but instead found four camouflaged E-boats clustered around the jetty. His attack was immediately followed by his wingman, F/L J.D. Younie, a recent arrival from 241 Squadron. Intense flak came from the E-boats and McCaig's Mustang was hit. The formation broke away as the Mustang began trailing white smoke. McCaig could not continue like this for long, so chose to bale out into the sea. He was eventually captured and spent what remained of the war as a prisoner. March started in a very bad way with F/L Muir shot down and killed while attacking a train a few miles south of Varaždin. He was seen to go straight into the ground, from a height of about 40 feet, and exploded. The squadron flew ops on a daily basis and no further losses were reported until the 16th when Lt P.E. Hill (SAAF) was posted missing on return from a bombing sortie on gun positions on the island of Rab. Indeed, on the return journey he reported his engine was running rough. Flight Sergeant E.J. Clarke was ordered to escort him to Ancona, the nearest airfield, but Hill soon reported he was losing oil pressure. He decided to bale out over the Adriatic and was seen to safely do so by Clarke. The latter orbited where Hill had gone down in the sea and saw him in his Mae West moving in the water, but did not see the dinghy. Clarke then flew to a small motorboat about a mile away and then back to Hill, to indicate where he was, but, on going back, Hill had disappeared. Nothing was ever seen or heard from Hill despite intense searches. It was his first operational sortie. In March, the main targets were trains. These operations could be dangerous as F/Sgt W.J. Monkman could attest. The train Monkman and Sgt E.A. Beer, his wingman, attacked was found near Darventa with 30 wagons. Some wagons were carrying oil drums while others were loaded with ammunition. Soon after the first burst, there was a huge explosion with a mass of flames rising to a thousand feet or more. Monkman immediately broke away from the danger zone, but it was too late as debris hit his aircraft. The aircraft soon proved to be too damaged to make it home so Monkman decided to bale out. He was saved by Chetniks who, while they did not hand over him to the Germans, kept him in custody until a short skirmish between them and partisans led to his liberation. On 24 March, 249 changed roles slightly and, in company with 213 Squadron, attacked the well-defended airfield at Gornji Stupnik in the Zagreb area. The attack was made from behind the cover of a hill, the aircraft climbing over it and swooping down

Pilots discuss tactics with S/L Edmondson (right) before a strafing sortie over Yugoslavia in February 1945. Left to right: F/Sgt J.R. Davie (RAF), F/O D.P. McCaig (Suva, Fiji), and F/Sgt E.J. Clarke (an Irishman).

to the deck. The formation employed was line abreast, each aircraft maintaining its course and firing directly ahead. Two Fw190s were claimed as destroyed and one Ju88 and one unidentified aircraft were claimed as damaged. No loss was reported. Otherwise, the squadron encountered considerable success against trains in March (during which more than 230 sorties were flown). There was no pause for 249 in April as it continued to harass German troops as other targets became rare. On 4 April, F/O E. Geddes, while leading an armed recce over the Jasenovac-Brod-Doboj area, spotted an aircraft that he initially thought could be an addition to the squadron's score. It was a biplane, but he soon discovered it was a Russian U-2. A few days later, on 11 April, the same pilot had another Russian encounter, this time with a MiG fighter, and, as with the U-2, nothing happened. The same day, F/O Gardner was hit in the coolant system while attacking MTs near Zepec. Forced to bale out, he was back the next day. A few days later, 249 was ready to make a move to Bari by road and the airfield of Prkos, near Zadar, in Yugoslavia. Due to a critical shortage of Mustangs at the time, the unit had to hand over its aircraft to 213 Squadron and was re-equipped with Spitfire IXs. The last Mustang sorties were flown on the 13th with two armed recces flown in the morning and the afternoon. The Mustangs the squadron had on charge in April were FB306/C, FB327/S, FB328/X, HB853, HB869/W, HB907/G, HB921, KH520/B, KH594/Y, KH606 and KH640/T. The association with the Mustang was not over, however, as, on 17 May 1945, the war now over, 249 returned to Biferno where it again converted to the Mustang. Two Mustang IIIs (FB328 and KH640), still carrying their 249 codes, were used to convert pilots who had experience on type before thirteen brand new Mk.IVs were taken on charge (see *SQUADRONS! 11*). Five Mustang IIIs were also received (FB145, HB948, KH424/V, KH512/U and HB921/C) in June. They were used until 249 disbanded on 18 August.

Claims - 249 Squadron (Confirmed and Probable)

Date	Pilot	SN	Origin	Type	Serial	Code	Nb	Cat.
31.10.44	F/L Peter F. **NOBLE**	CAN./ J.19165	RCAF	Fi156	**KH427**	GN-V	0.5	C
	F/O John **DICKERSON**	RAF No. 150325	RAF		**KH575**	GN-Z	0.5	C
	Total: 1.0							

Mustang III KH427/GN-V participated in 249 Squadron's final aerial claim of the war on 31 October 1944 when flown by F/L P.F. Noble RCAF. This Mustang is still wearing Fighter Command markings with Sky spinner and fuselage band.
(Andrew Thomas)

Date	Pilot	S/N	Origin	Serial	Code	Fate
13.09.44	2/Lt William **Shields**	SAAF No. 542523	SAAF	**HB926**		-
21.09.44	Sgt Alfred W. **Manning**	RAF No. 520864	RAF	**KH422**		**Inj.**
22.09.44	F/L Alfred E. **Dryden**	NZ413549	RNZAF	**KH468**		†
	Capt Richard T. **Whittingham**	SAAF No. 328957	SAAF	**KH425**		**Eva.**
27.09.44	F/Sgt Edgar **Ray**	Aus. 410380	RAAF	**KH476**		†
08.10.44	F/O Dennis P.F. **McCaig** [1]	RAF No. 155772	RAF	**HB933**	GN-X	**Eva.**
16.10.44	Capt Richard T. **Whittingham**	SAAF No. 328957	SAAF	**KH532**		-
19.10.44	W/O Cyril N.V. **Davey**	RAF No. 1314003	RAF	**KH428**		†
	P/O Robert **Andrew**	RAF No. 177539	RAF	**KH530**		**Eva.**
24.10.44	Lt Horace K. **Rachmann**	SAAF No. 542521	SAAF	**HB941**		†
30.10.44	Sgt Hammond G. **Pallett**	RAF No. 1399270	RAF	**KH437**		†
12.11.44	Sgt James R. **Davie**	RAF No. 975092	RAF	**KH568**	GN-H	-
24.11.44	Sgt Peter W. **Amis**	RAF No. 1804379	RAF	**HB928**	GN-A	-
01.12.44	Sgt Walter M. **Monkman**	RAF No. 1458458	RAF	**HB884**	GN-D	-
02.12.44	Sgt Frederick J. **Weed**	RAF No. 1602764	RAF	**KH472**	GN-E	**PoW**
27.12.44	F/Sgt Maurice **Smith**	RAF No. 1622474	RAF	**FB330**		**Eva.**
29.12.44	F/O John W. **Gardner**	RAF No. 152022	RAF	**KH543**	GN-F	-
26.01.45	F/Sgt Peter C. **Jones**	RAF No. 1335888	RAF	**HB883**		-
02.02.45	Lt Raymond V. **Jacobs**	SAAF No. 328838	SAAF	**FB308**	GN-E	†
26.02.45	F/O Dennis P.F. **McCaig**	RAF No. 155772	RAF	**HB912**	GN-A	**PoW**
01.03.45	F/L John R. **Muir** [2]	RAF No. 150307	RAF	**HB851**		†
16.03.45	Lt Peter E. **Hill**	SAAF No. 178036	SAAF	**HB859**		†
20.03.45	Sgt Walter M. **Monkman**	RAF No. 1458458	RAF	**KH619**	GN-H	**Eva.**
11.04.45	F/O John W. **Gardner**	RAF No. 152022	RAF	**FB327**	GN-S	-

Total: 24

[1] *From Fiji*

[2] *From the Channel Islands*

Sgt J.R. Davie posing in front of its Mustang KH568/GN-H with which he experienced a take-off accident on 12 November 1944. He escaped unscratched but got luck in not seeing the two bombs under the wings to explode.

WITH NOS. 250 AND 450 SQUADRONS

When the war ended in the region, various fighter units operating over the Balkans or over Italy were scheduled to convert to the Mustang IV (occasionally supplemented by Mk. IIIs).

No. 250 (Sudan) Squadron, code LD

This was another unit that used Kittyhawks for a long time, but the war came to an end before it could re-equip with Mustangs. Shortly after VE-Day the squadron passed under S/L P.J.B. Bagshawe's command. He had been awarded the DFC the previous March for his actions with 250. The squadron moved to Lavariano, its peacetime base, and conversion began to take place in August as the turnover of pilots gathered pace as many units in the zone disbanded. The final Kittyhawk flights were performed on 13 August and the same day Mustangs were taxied over from 260 Squadron and fitters and riggers were soon busy understanding the intricacies of the new machines, a mixed force of Mk.IIIs and IVs (among them Mk.IIIs FB298, HB922, HB945, KH561, KH575, KH595, KH583 and KH597). The first practice flights were undertaken two days later. The redeployment of pilots continued. In September, training was carried on with RP launchers, a weapon never used by operational Mustang squadrons since the introduction of the type in the RAF. A total of 164 rockets were eventually fired in September. On 2 October, the first mishap was recorded when Sgt Moody developed engine trouble and was compelled to crash land at Vicenza landing ground. While Moody escaped injury, the Mustang was only good for scrap. After 289 hours flown in September, the squadron added another 240 in October. This was accompanied with a move to their winter quarters at Mortegliano village. The bad weather at the end of 1945 made for difficult flying and only 35 hours were logged. The squadron settled into a routine in 1946 (with a crash on 15 August caused by a glycol leak setting fire to the aircraft, the pilot managed to make an emergency landing). This continued until the squadron was disbanded in January 1947. The Mustang IIIs known to have been used by 250 are FB334, HB952, HB960, HB961, KH522, KH538 and KH597.

Summary of the aircraft lost by accident - 250 Squadron

Date	Pilot	S/N	Origin	Serial	Code	Fate
02.10.45	Sgt Ronald G.M. **Moody**	RAF No. 1608078	RAF	**KH522**		-
		Total: 1				

250 Sqn had the distinction of becoming the only RAF Mustang unit to be equipped with RP launchers (never used on ops). *(Andrew Thomas)*

Left, LD-B seen at Treviso in 1946. *(Andrew Thomas)*

Below:
A line-up of Mustang IIIs in the snow at Montegliano village (Tissano) in March 1946 (LD-E and LD-D visible). Note the Mustang on the left with the engine cowlings off and rockets on the rails. *(AHM of WA)*

Bottom, Mustang LD-Y fitted with rocket mounts.

No. 450 (RAAF) Squadron, code OK:

When the war ended in Italy, the squadron was about to exchange its Kittyhawk Mk. IVs for Mustangs. This process seems to have been stopped early and never completed as the squadron, like other Australian units located in Italy or the Mediterranean, was intended for disbandment or, at least, the majority of its personnel repatriated. The number of Mustangs issued to the squadron is uncertain but about half a dozen are clearly identified and included one Mk. III (FB244/OK-F). The squadron therefore flew Mk. IIIs and the Mk. IV until disbandment on 24 August 1945. Whatever the number, the hours flown were low as daily work concentrated on preparing personnel for repatriation. All of the aircraft were handed over to No. 380 MU aircraft storage unit at Campoformido.

The two sides of the very battered and touched up 450 Sqn Mustang FB244/OK-F. *(AHW of WA)*

North American Mustang Mk. III KH631
No. 3 Squadron, RAAF
Fano (Italy), winter 1944-1945

North American Mustang Mk. III FB128
No. 3 Squadron, RAAF
Lavariano (Italy), summer 1945

North American Mustang Mk. III KH610
No. 5 Squadron, SAAF
Cervia (Italy), spring 1945

Donald James Matthew BLAKESLEE DFC

Supermarine Spitfire Mk.VB EN951
No. 133 (Eagle) Squadron
Flight Lieutenant D. J. M. Blakeslee
CAN./ J-4551
Gravesend (UK) August 1942

Charles Cuthbertson LEARMONTH DFC*

Douglas Boston Mk. III A28-9/41x-AL8911
No. 22 Squadron RAAF
Squadron Leader C. C. Learmonth
Aus. 385
Port Moresby (New Guinea), spring 1943

Hans Anton MAURENBRECHER

Curtiss P-40N-35-CU C3-560
No. 120 (NEI) Squadron
Major H. Maurenbrecher
Biak (New Guinea), 1945-1946

Roland Prosper BEAMONT DSO* DFC*

Hawker Tempest Mk V JN751
No. 150 Wing
Wing Commander R. P. Beamont
RAF No. 41819
Bradwell Bay (UK), April 1944

Ronald Thomas SUSANS DSO DFC

North American P-51D-25-NT A68-724
No. 77 squadron, RAAF
Squadron Leader R. T. Susans
O43391
Bofu (Japan), 1947

James Henry LACEY DFM*

Supermarine Spitfire Mk.XIV RN135
No. 17 Squadron
Squadron Leader J. H. Lacey
RAF No. 112709
Seletar (Singapore), autumn 1945

Introducing's RAF In Combat and Bravo Bravo Aviation's collection of
highly-detailed and historically accurate, high-quality aviation prints.
For more information on available prints, please visit :

www.raf-in-combat.com   or

Bravo Bravo Aviation
BBA
HIGH QUALITY AVIATION ILLUSTRATION
www.BravoBravoAviation.com

Brian Alexander EATON DSO*, DFC

North American Mustang Mk. III FB260
No. 239 Wing
Group Captain B. Eaton
Aus. 133
Italy, autumn 1944

Prints in connection with the book:

PL-035: B.A. Eaton
PL-203: T.C. MacMurray
PL-204: J. Te Kloot
PL-205: C.E. Edmondson